Follow the Stars

A Native American Woodlands Tale

Retold and Illustrated by

Kristina Rodanas

MARSHALL CAVENDISH
New York

For Sheri, who listens with her heart

And for Kate, the Brave One

—*K. R.*

Marshall Cavendish, 99 White Plains Road, Tarrytown, New York 10591

Library of Congress Cataloging-in-Publication Data
Rodanas, Kristina. Follow the stars : a native American woodlands tale / retold and illustrated by Kristina Rodanas. — 1st ed.
p.   cm. Summary: A journey made across snowbound lands by animals in search of the missing Birds of Summer results in the return of the warm season.
ISBN 0-7614-5029-7 (hc)
1. Ojibwa Indians — Folklore. [1. Summer — Folklore. 2. Ojibwa Indians — Folklore. 3. Indians of North America — Folklore.
4. Folklore — North America.]
E99.C6R632   1998   398.2'089'973 — [E]—DC20   95-7103   CIP   AC

The paintings were done in colored pencil over watercolor wash. The text is set in 14 point Garamond Book.

First edition. Printed in Italy.

1 3 5 6 4 2

Author's Note

There are many tales from the Eastern Woodlands storytelling tradition that recall the resourcefulness of a group of animals who bring the warmth of summer to their homelands. In several of these stories, the animals are led by the fisher, a brave, clever mammal similar to a mink, and encounter a manitou, an important spirit who is believed to inhabit all elements of the natural world. *Follow the Stars* is based on these stories, including an Ojibwa tale entitled "Ojeeg Annung," by Henry R. Schoolcraft, originally published by Harper Brothers in 1839. I hope that this tale will speak to the hearts of all who are willing to listen.

It was I, the Quiet One, who was chosen to watch and to listen so that one day I could tell you this story. Many years have gone by since the time of the Everlasting Snow. I remember the winter sky was dark with clouds. Heavy snow covered the hills and fields, and the rivers had turned to ice. The wind howled like a hundred hungry wolves....

The animals of the forest waited for winter to melt as it always had before. But the warm winds never came to chase away the cold. When all their stored food was eaten and the last of the withered plants had been dug up from beneath the snow, their hearts froze with fear.

"Where is summer?" they asked one another. "What will happen if winter never ends?"

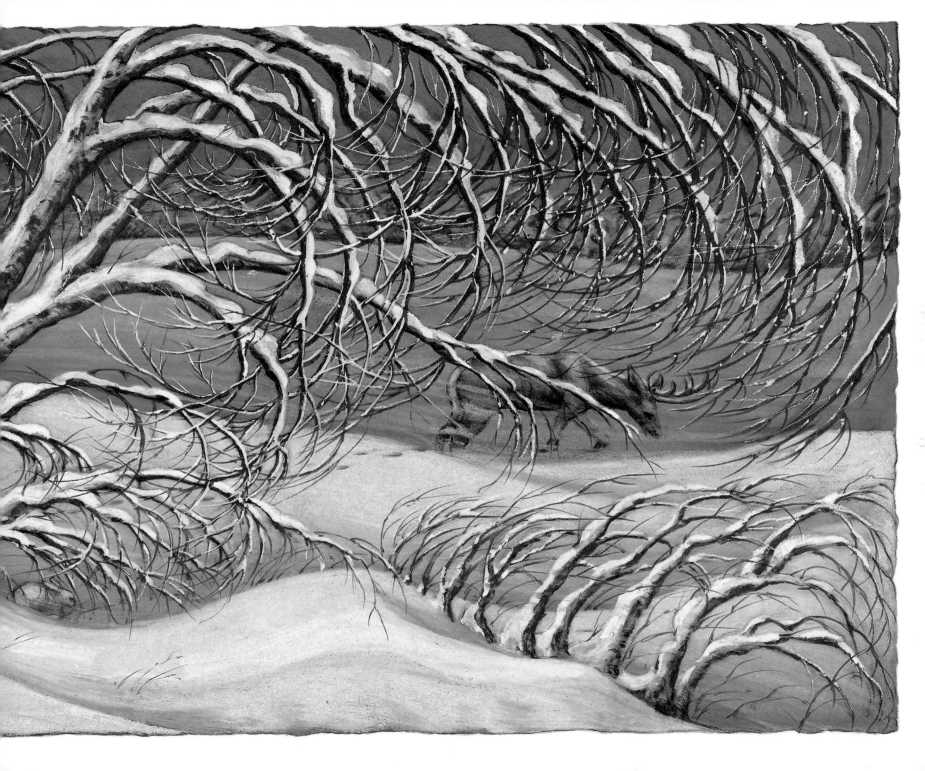

Moose, the biggest and strongest of the animals, called a meeting. Beaver, Gray Fox, Field Mouse, Lynx, Rabbit, Timber Wolf, and all the others shivered beneath the rising moon.

Wise Fisher was the last to arrive. He listened as his friends talked of their hardships. When their voices grew so loud with fear that the snow shook free from the trees, he stood and spoke.

"I think I know why summer has not yet come," he said. "Each year when the birds fly away, the birch leaves turn yellow and fall to the earth. New green leaves appear only when the birds return. But this year, the birds of summer have not come back to us. When they return, summer will follow."

"But what has become of them?" Wolverine growled.

Fisher gazed upward into the night sky. He pricked his ears forward and cocked his head. At last he said, "Someone has captured the birds of summer. We must find them and set them free."

Moose snorted. "Indeed! Who has put this foolish thought in your head?" he said.

Fisher lowered his eyes. "The stars have told me. They will guide me and all who follow to the birds of summer."

"The stars!" Moose stamped his hoof. "Why have these points of light in the sky never spoken to me?" He turned to the others. "Have they spoken to you?"

The animals all shook their heads. Then Timber Wolf said, "But if Fisher is right, what have we to lose by following him? If we do nothing, we will surely die of the cold."

So the animals agreed to leave that very night. Fisher led the way, following a white belt of stars that stretched across the dark horizon. They slept only when the stars melted into the gray sky of dawn.

After many nights of journeying, they reached the foot of a towering mountain.

Tired and hungry, some of the animals wondered if they should turn back.

"We have gained nothing from this journey," Moose grumbled. "Fisher's phantom voices have only led us to lands as snowbound as those we left behind."

Yet as Fisher led them up the mountain, the air became warmer. Thin streams of melted snow trickled through the rocks. Encouraged, they continued upward.

At the summit, the animals peered down into a moonlit valley full of blooming flowers, leafy trees, and strange dwellings. All was silent but for soft cooing sounds that rose from below.

"They are here," Fisher whispered. Quickly and quietly, he led the animals down the mountainside.

JACOBSVILLE ELEMENTARY SCHOOL

Suddenly the valley came to life. Strange two-legged creatures dressed in the skins of animals heaped wood onto a fire and danced in the place where summer never ends.

"What kind of animals are these?" wondered Gray Fox. "They have taken the furs of our sisters and brothers and kept summer all to themselves!"

"We will never defeat such dangerous creatures. Summer is lost to us forever!" Moose said.

Fisher looked from one frightened face to the next. "Each of us alone would not have the strength to face them. But if we join our hearts and minds together, we will be strong enough to set the birds of summer free."

They waited until the two-leggeds had returned to their huts. Shoulder to shoulder and nose to tail, the animals moved as a single creature into the sleeping village. With their many voices, they snorted, snarled, barked, and howled.

The two-leggeds ran from their wigwams. The awesome beast before them struck terror into their hearts. "Manitou! Manitou!" they cried, pointing at Fisher and the others. "A powerful spirit is angry with us! Run, quickly!" Within minutes, the village was empty.

From inside the wigwams, beautiful birdsongs echoed. "Release the birds of summer!" cried Fisher. "Hurry! We must be gone before the two-legged creatures return!"

The animals ran from lodge to lodge, tearing open the cages they found within. Graceful swallows flew from one basket, and colorful finches poured out of the next. Then came robins, warblers, woodpeckers, and jays.

Flocks of swans and clouds of hummingbirds flashed in the firelight.

As a rainbow of birds rose into the sky, the warm winds of summer followed, breathing new life into the snow-covered land.

Behind them, an icy frost settled over the valley. Fisher called to the others, "Do not wait for me! Follow the birds and see that their path is safe. Listen to the stars! I will open the last of the cages. Then I will join you!"

The animals gazed into the night sky. Far above the fading birdsongs, they heard the whispers of the stars, guiding them safely home.

Just as Fisher released a wave of bluebirds, the people returned. They charged at him. For an instant, Fisher froze. Then he dashed between their long legs and ran for his life.

He darted toward the forest but could not escape the angry creatures who followed closely behind. In desperation, Fisher leaped into a tall tree and scrambled all the way to the top. Only the sky remained above him.

Trembling, he looked down at his pursuers. Then he heard the stars whisper, "Brave Fisher, come. Be one of us. Jump high!"

Stretching out his paws, Fisher sprang from the treetop and, like an eagle, soared high into the night.

When the rest of the animals reached their homes, summer had returned at last.

But where was Fisher? They searched many days but could find no trace of him. One night, under a rising moon, they gathered to talk of his wisdom and bravery. With sadness in their hearts, they wondered if they would ever see their friend again.

"Perhaps we should ask the stars if they have seen him," Moose suggested quietly.

The animals looked up at the flickering stars and saw Fisher dancing among them. They heard a whisper, "I will always be your friend. Look to me to guide you."

It has been this way ever since. When the birds of summer fly far away, the birch leaves turn yellow. But year after year, the birds come back to us, melting the cold with the warmth that follows them. Brave Fisher shines bright in the night sky and is always there to show them the way home. This is how I remember it. It is a story the stars whisper to those who listen.